# I COULDN'T DEC WHAT TO GET YOU SO... I GOT YOU A BOOK FULL OF COUPONS!

**THIS COUPON ENTITLES YOU TO**

play with boobies

**TERMS & CONDITIONS:**
CAN BE REDEEMED AT ANY TIME. THE COUPON HOLDER MUST HAVE AT LEAST 15 MIN BOOB PLAY. NON-TRANSFERABLE.

*Enjoy!*

**THIS COUPON ENTITLES YOU TO**

play with boobies

**TERMS & CONDITIONS:**
CAN BE REDEEMED AT ANY TIME. THE COUPON HOLDER MUST HAVE AT LEAST 15 MIN BOOB PLAY. NON-TRANSFERABLE.

# THIS COUPON ENTITLES YOU TO A

# massage and a happy ending

## TERMS & CONDITIONS:

CAN BE REDEEMED ONLY ON WEEKENDS,
NOT WEEK DAYS. THE COUPON HOLDER
MUST BE IN THEIR OWN BED.
NON-TRANSFERABLE.

# brea CRUSH

coupons for every occasion

# THIS COUPON ENTITLES YOU TO A

# massage and a happy ending

**TERMS & CONDITIONS:**
CAN BE REDEEMED ONLY ON WEEKENDS,
NOT WEEK DAYS. THE COUPON HOLDER
MUST BE IN THEIR OWN BED.
NON-TRANSFERABLE.

0000000000000000

# brea
# CRUSH

coupons for every occasion

# THIS COUPON ENTITLES YOU TO A

# chore free weekend

**TERMS & CONDITIONS:**
CAN BE REDEEMED ONLY AT WEEKENDS.
VALID ON SATURDAYS AND SUNDAYS.
NON-TRANSFERABLE.

0000000000000000

brea
CRUSH
coupons for every occasion

# THIS COUPON ENTITLES YOU TO A

# chore free weekend

**TERMS & CONDITIONS:**
CAN BE REDEEMED ONLY AT WEEKENDS.
VALID ON SATURDAYS AND SUNDAYS.
NON-TRANSFERABLE.

0000000000000000

# brea CRUSH

coupons for every occasion

# THIS COUPON ENTITLES YOU TO A

# quickie

## TERMS & CONDITIONS:

CAN BE REDEEMED AT A TIME & PLACE OF
YOUR CHOICE. THE COUPON HOLDER MUST
HAVE SHOWERED WITHIN AN HOUR & MUST
BE STD FREE. NON-TRANSFERABLE.

0000000000000000

# brea CRUSH

coupons for every occasion

# THIS COUPON ENTITLES YOU TO A

# quickie

## TERMS & CONDITIONS:

CAN BE REDEEMED AT A TIME & PLACE OF YOUR CHOICE. THE COUPON HOLDER MUST HAVE SHOWERED WITHIN AN HOUR & MUST BE STD FREE. NON-TRANSFERABLE.

0000000000000000

# brea
# CRUSH
coupons for every occasion

# THIS COUPON ENTITLES YOU TO A

# cuddle session

## TERMS & CONDITIONS:
CAN BE REDEEMED AT ANY TIME &
ANYWHERE. NON-TRANSFERABLE.

0000000000000000

# brea
# CRUSH

coupons for every occasion

# THIS COUPON ENTITLES YOU TO A

# cuddle session

**TERMS & CONDITIONS:**
CAN BE REDEEMED AT ANY TIME & ANYWHERE. NON-TRANSFERABLE.

0000000000000000

# brea CRUSH

coupons for every occasion

# THIS COUPON ENTITLES YOU TO

# one sexy wish

## TERMS & CONDITIONS:

CAN BE REDEEMED AT ANYTIME.
THE COUPON HOLDER CAN HAVE
1 WISH OF THEIR CHOOSING.
NON-TRANSFERABLE.

# brea
# CRUSH
coupons for every occasion

# THIS COUPON ENTITLES YOU TO

# one
# sexy wish

### TERMS & CONDITIONS:
CAN BE REDEEMED AT ANYTIME.
THE COUPON HOLDER CAN HAVE
1 WISH OF THEIR CHOOSING.
NON-TRANSFERABLE.

0000000000000000

# brea
# CRUSH

coupons for every occasion

# THIS COUPON ENTITLES YOU TO

# shower sex

### TERMS & CONDITIONS:
CAN BE REDEEMED AT ANY TIME.
THE COUPON HOLDER MUST HAVE NOT
SHOWERED ON THAT DAY ALREADY.
NON-TRANSFERABLE.

# THIS COUPON ENTITLES YOU TO

# shower
# sex

### TERMS & CONDITIONS:
CAN BE REDEEMED AT ANY TIME.
THE COUPON HOLDER MUST HAVE NOT
SHOWERED ON THAT DAY ALREADY.
NON-TRANSFERABLE.

brea
CRUSH
coupons for every occasion

# THIS COUPON ENTITLES YOU TO

# morning
# sex

## TERMS & CONDITIONS:
CAN BE REDEEMED ONLY AT WEEKENDS.
THE COUPON HOLDER MUST HAVE
SHOWERED WITHIN AN HOUR.
NON-TRANSFERABLE.

# brea
# CRUSH
coupons for every occasion

# THIS COUPON ENTITLES YOU TO

## morning sex

### TERMS & CONDITIONS:
CAN BE REDEEMED ONLY AT WEEKENDS.
THE COUPON HOLDER MUST HAVE
SHOWERED WITHIN AN HOUR.
NON-TRANSFERABLE.

0000000000000000

# brea
# CRUSH
coupons for every occasion

# THIS COUPON ENTITLES YOU TO

# daytime fun

### TERMS & CONDITIONS:

CAN BE REDEEMED ONLY IN DAY TIME. THE
COUPON HOLDER HAS THE CHOICE OF ANY
ROLE PLAYNG THAT THEY WISH.
NON-TRANSFERABLE.

0000000000000000

# brea
# CRUSH
coupons for every occasion

# THIS COUPON ENTITLES YOU TO

# daytime fun

### TERMS & CONDITIONS:
CAN BE REDEEMED ONLY IN DAY TIME. THE
COUPON HOLDER HAS THE CHOICE OF ANY
ROLE PLAYNG THAT THEY WISH.
NON-TRANSFERABLE.

# brea CRUSH

coupons for every occasion

# THIS COUPON ENTITLES YOU TO A

# blowjob

## TERMS & CONDITIONS:

CAN BE REDEEMED AT A TIME & PLACE OF
YOUR CHOICE. THE COUPON HOLDER MUST
HAVE SHOWERED WITHIN AN HOUR & MUST
BE STD FREE NON-TRANSFERABLE.

0000000000000000

# THIS COUPON ENTITLES YOU TO A

# blowjob

### TERMS & CONDITIONS:
CAN BE REDEEMED AT A TIME & PLACE OF
YOUR CHOICE. THE COUPON HOLDER MUST
HAVE SHOWERED WITHIN AN HOUR & MUST
BE STD FREE NON-TRANSFERABLE.

0000000000000000

# brea CRUSH

coupons for every occasion

# THIS COUPON ENTITLES YOU TO

# breakfast in bed

### TERMS & CONDITIONS:

CAN BE REDEEMED ONLY AT WEEKENDS.
THE COUPON HOLDER CAN HAVE ANY
BREAKFAST OF THEIR CHOOSING.
NON-TRANSFERABLE.

0000000000000000

# brea
# CRUSH

coupons for every occasion

# THIS COUPON ENTITLES YOU TO

# breakfast in bed

## TERMS & CONDITIONS:
CAN BE REDEEMED ONLY AT WEEKENDS.
THE COUPON HOLDER CAN HAVE ANY
BREAKFAST OF THEIR CHOOSING.
NON-TRANSFERABLE.

0000000000000000

# brea
## CRUSH
coupons for every occasion

# THIS COUPON ENTITLES YOU TO

# make up sex

## TERMS & CONDITIONS:

CAN BE REDEEMED AT A TIME & PLACE OF
YOUR CHOICE. THE COUPON HOLDER MUST
HAVE SHOWERED WITHIN AN HOUR & MUST
BE STD FREE. NON-TRANSFERABLE.

0000000000000000

# brea
# CRUSH
coupons for every occasion

# THIS COUPON ENTITLES YOU TO

# make up sex

## TERMS & CONDITIONS:

CAN BE REDEEMED AT A TIME & PLACE OF YOUR CHOICE. THE COUPON HOLDER MUST HAVE SHOWERED WITHIN AN HOUR & MUST BE STD FREE. NON-TRANSFERABLE.

0000000000000000

brea
CRUSH
coupons for every occasion

# THIS COUPON ENTITLES YOU TO A

# tie-up

## TERMS & CONDITIONS:

CAN BE REDEEMED ONLY AT NIGHT TIME.
THE COUPON HOLDER HAS THE CHOICE OF
GIVING OR RECEIVING THE TIE-UP.
NON-TRANSFERABLE.

# brea CRUSH

coupons for every occasion

# THIS COUPON ENTITLES YOU TO A

# tie-up

### TERMS & CONDITIONS:

CAN BE REDEEMED ONLY AT NIGHT TIME.
THE COUPON HOLDER HAS THE CHOICE OF
GIVING OR RECEIVING THE TIE-UP.
NON-TRANSFERABLE.

0000000000000000

# brea
# CRUSH
coupons for every occasion

# THIS COUPON ENTITLES YOU TO A

# naked
# house keeper

**TERMS & CONDITIONS:**
CAN BE REDEEMED ONLY DURING THE DAY.
THE COUPON HOLDER MUST HAVE THEIR
WIFE / GF BE THE HOUSE KEEPER.
NON-TRANSFERABLE.

# brea CRUSH

coupons for every occasion

# THIS COUPON ENTITLES YOU TO A

# naked
# house keeper

**TERMS & CONDITIONS:**
CAN BE REDEEMED ONLY DURING THE DAY.
THE COUPON HOLDER MUST HAVE THEIR
WIFE / GF BE THE HOUSE KEEPER.
NON-TRANSFERABLE.

0000000000000000

# brea CRUSH

coupons for every occasion

# THIS COUPON ENTITLES YOU TO

# phone
# sex

## TERMS & CONDITIONS:
CAN BE REDEEMED AT ANY TIME.
THE COUPON HOLDER CAN CHOOSE A TXT
OR A PHONE CALL. NON-TRANSFERABLE.

# THIS COUPON ENTITLES YOU TO

# phone sex

## TERMS & CONDITIONS:
CAN BE REDEEMED AT ANY TIME.
THE COUPON HOLDER CAN CHOOSE A TXT
OR A PHONE CALL. NON-TRANSFERABLE.

0000000000000000

# brea CRUSH

coupons for every occasion

# THIS COUPON ENTITLES YOU TO A

# sexual fantasy

### TERMS & CONDITIONS:
CAN BE REDEEMED ONLY AT NIGHT TIME.
THE COUPON HOLDER CAN HAVE ANY
SEXUAL FANTASY THAT THEY DESIRE.
NON-TRANSFERABLE.

brea
CRUSH
coupons for every occasion

# THIS COUPON ENTITLES YOU TO A

## sexual fantasy

### TERMS & CONDITIONS:
CAN BE REDEEMED ONLY AT NIGHT TIME.
THE COUPON HOLDER CAN HAVE ANY
SEXUAL FANTASY THAT THEY DESIRE.
NON-TRANSFERABLE.

# brea
# CRUSH

coupons for every occasion

# THIS COUPON ENTITLES YOU TO

# control of the tv for 24 hours

**TERMS & CONDITIONS:**
CAN BE REDEEMED ONLY ON THE COUCH.
THE COUPON HOLDER CAN EVEN WATCH
XRATED CONTENT.
NON-TRANSFERABLE.

0000000000000000

# THIS COUPON ENTITLES YOU TO

# control of the tv for 24 hours

## TERMS & CONDITIONS:
CAN BE REDEEMED ONLY ON THE COUCH.
THE COUPON HOLDER CAN EVEN WATCH
XRATED CONTENT.
NON-TRANSFERABLE.

0000000000000000

# brea
# CRUSH
coupons for every occasion

# THIS COUPON ENTITLES YOU TO A

## quickie in the
## kitchen

**TERMS & CONDITIONS:**

CAN BE REDEEMED AT ANY TIME.
THE COUPON HOLDER MUST HAVE
SHOWERED WITHIN AN HOUR.
NON-TRANSFERABLE.

brea
CRUSH
coupons for every occasion

# THIS COUPON ENTITLES YOU TO A

# quickie in the kitchen

**TERMS & CONDITIONS:**

CAN BE REDEEMED AT ANY TIME.
THE COUPON HOLDER MUST HAVE
SHOWERED WITHIN AN HOUR.
NON-TRANSFERABLE.

# brea
# CRUSH
coupons for every occasion

# THIS COUPON ENTITLES YOU TO

# 3 wishes

## TERMS & CONDITIONS:

CAN BE REDEEMED AT ANY TIME. THE
COUPON HOLDER GET'S A CHOICE OF 3
WISHES. MUST CHOOSE CAREFULLY!
NON-TRANSFERABLE.

# THIS COUPON ENTITLES YOU TO

# 3 wishes

### TERMS & CONDITIONS:

CAN BE REDEEMED AT ANY TIME. THE
COUPON HOLDER GET'S A CHOICE OF 3
WISHES. MUST CHOOSE CAREFULLY!
NON-TRANSFERABLE.

0000000000000000

# brea
# CRUSH
coupons for every occasion

# THIS COUPON ENTITLES YOU TO A

# sexy
# lap dance

## TERMS & CONDITIONS:
CAN BE REDEEMED ONLY AT NIGHT TIME.
THE COUPON HOLDER MUST ALSO BE NAKED
FOR THE DANCE. NON-TRANSFERABLE.

# THIS COUPON ENTITLES YOU TO A

# sexy
# lap dance

## TERMS & CONDITIONS:
CAN BE REDEEMED ONLY AT NIGHT TIME.
THE COUPON HOLDER MUST ALSO BE NAKED
FOR THE DANCE. NON-TRANSFERABLE.

brea
CRUSH
coupons for every occasion

# THIS COUPON ENTITLES YOU TO

# car fun

### TERMS & CONDITIONS:

CAN BE REDEEMED AT ANY TIME.
THE COUPON HOLDER OR GF / WIFE
MUST HAVE A CAR. NON-TRANSFERABLE.

0000000000000000

# THIS COUPON ENTITLES YOU TO

# car fun

### TERMS & CONDITIONS:
CAN BE REDEEMED AT ANY TIME.
THE COUPON HOLDER OR GF / WIFE
MUST HAVE A CAR. NON-TRANSFERABLE.

0000000000000000

# brea
# CRUSH
coupons for every occasion

# THIS COUPON ENTITLES YOU TO A

# naked
# chef

## TERMS & CONDITIONS:

CAN BE REDEEMED ONLY DURING THE DAY.
THE COUPON HOLDER CAN HAVE ANYTHING
THAT THEY DESIRE COOKED FOR THEM.
NON-TRANSFERABLE.

0000000000000000

# THIS COUPON ENTITLES YOU TO A

# naked chef

## TERMS & CONDITIONS:

CAN BE REDEEMED ONLY DURING THE DAY.
THE COUPON HOLDER CAN HAVE ANYTHING
THAT THEY DESIRE COOKED FOR THEM.
NON-TRANSFERABLE.

# brea
# CRUSH
coupons for every occasion

# THIS COUPON ENTITLES YOU TO

## oral pleasure

**TERMS & CONDITIONS:**

CAN BE REDEEMED ONLY DURING THE DAY.
THE COUPON MUST BE CLEAN AND
SHOWERED IN THE LAST HOUR.
NON-TRANSFERABLE.

0000000000000000

# brea
# CRUSH
coupons for every occasion

# THIS COUPON ENTITLES YOU TO

# oral pleasure

## TERMS & CONDITIONS:
CAN BE REDEEMED ONLY DURING THE DAY.
THE COUPON MUST BE CLEAN AND
SHOWERED IN THE LAST HOUR.
NON-TRANSFERABLE.

0000000000000000

# brea CRUSH

coupons for every occasion

# THIS COUPON ENTITLES YOU TO A

# new position

## TERMS & CONDITIONS:
CAN BE REDEEMED ONLY AT NIGHT TIME.
THE COUPON HOLDER TRY A NEW SEX
POSITION OF THEIR CHOOSING.
NON-TRANSFERABLE.

# THIS COUPON ENTITLES YOU TO A

# new position

### TERMS & CONDITIONS:

CAN BE REDEEMED ONLY AT NIGHT TIME.
THE COUPON HOLDER TRY A NEW SEX
POSITION OF THEIR CHOOSING.
NON-TRANSFERABLE.

0000000000000000

# brea
# CRUSH
coupons for every occasion

# THIS COUPON ENTITLES YOU TO

# play with boobies

## TERMS & CONDITIONS:
CAN BE REDEEMED AT ANY TIME. THE COUPON HOLDER MUST HAVE AT LEAST 15 MIN BOOB PLAY. NON-TRANSFERABLE.

0000000000000000

brea
CRUSH
coupons for every occasion

# THIS COUPON ENTITLES YOU TO

# play with boobies

## TERMS & CONDITIONS:

CAN BE REDEEMED AT ANY TIME. THE COUPON HOLDER MUST HAVE AT LEAST 15 MIN BOOB PLAY. NON-TRANSFERABLE.

0000000000000000

# brea CRUSH

coupons for every occasion

# THIS COUPON ENTITLES YOU TO A

# strip
# tease

## TERMS & CONDITIONS:
CAN BE REDEEMED ONLY AT NIGHT TIME.
THE COUPON HOLDER MUST BE NAKED FOR
THE STRIP TEASE. NON-TRANSFERABLE.

# THIS COUPON ENTITLES YOU TO A

## strip tease

### TERMS & CONDITIONS:
CAN BE REDEEMED ONLY AT NIGHT TIME.
THE COUPON HOLDER MUST BE NAKED FOR
THE STRIP TEASE. NON-TRANSFERABLE.

# brea
# CRUSH
coupons for every occasion

Printed in Great Britain
by Amazon

35045744R00057